Manhattanite

Reading Aaron Poochigian's *Manhattanite* is a dynamic, kinetic experience. These poems travel at a fast clip, pulling you along through cityscapes, wastelands, and other vistas. Some of the poems tunnel downward, plumbing depths of mood and memory. Whichever way they move, Poochigian's poems perform with such panache and brio that it's hard to know whether to laugh or cry. I'd say do both—and keep reading. In a dark time, *Manhattanite* will entertain you while also educating you about poetics and history and life. But be warned: this isn't a feel-good book. It's a fearless book.
— Rachel Hadas, author of *The River of Forgetfulness*

Like the shuttered diner that used to serve "Americana-for-the-budget-patron," *Manhattanite* gives us the Manhattan of speed chess players in the park, tipsy tipplers tipping off the rooftops, the night sky bright with city light, tenants, tenements and supers. The city of this book is populated with ghetto Socrates, Tarot kings, and gutter saints, sketched out in perfect metrical form that somehow captures the nuance of how we actually speak: "... and I was just, like, 'whoa.' / My brakes were freakin' screaming." Aaron Poochigian is the poet in New York seeking a holy aura in the song of gunshots and spiral sirens, picking like a grizzled pigeon through stray newspapers, bottles, bags, and candy wrappers for a scrap of religion. Each poem is a tower growing out of our human filth and scraping the sky with sky-lines, and together they build a city of words. Put New York in your pocket. It's inside this book.
— Tony Barnstone, author of *Pulp Sonnets*

Thoreau once boasted that he had traveled widely in Concord; Aaron Poochigian's title indicates that he has traveled widely elsewhere—in the one borough worth experiencing, through western deserts, aboard "an ultra-modern train/ lisping through French or German woods," and in a Paris of naked bulbs and seedy cabarets. In all of these settings, he deftly choreographs his cast of nameless characters, saying, "It's gorgeous how the tragic dance/ around us trailing shadows of tristesse." To say that these poems teem with life and wonderment seems a feckless understatement; *febrile* is the word that comes first to mind in attempting to describe their world of motion and emotion. The concluding lines of "Song: Go and Do It"(channeling both John Donne and The Intruders) claim, "I'll still swear/ we could be happy anywhere." One sure location of that "anywhere" exists between the covers of *Manhattanite*.

— R. S. Gwynn, author of *Dogwatch*

In *Manhattanite,* his second book of poems, Aaron Poochigian takes on the role of American flâneur for the twenty-first century, drifting through the frenetic metropolis at a dreamer's planetary pace. . . .

— A. E. Stallings (full text in the foreword on page ix),
2016 Able Muse Book Award judge, author of *Olives*

MANHATTANITE

POEMS BY
Aaron Poochigian

WINNER OF THE 2016 ABLE MUSE BOOK AWARD

ABLE MUSE PRESS

Able Muse Press

www.ablemusepress.com

Printed in the United States of America

Library of Congress Control Number: 2017930338

ISBN 978-1-927409-92-3 (paperback)
ISBN 978-1-927409-93-0 (digital)

Cover image: "Light Skywalking" by Alexander Pepple

Cover & book design by Alexander Pepple

Able Muse Press is an imprint of *Able Muse:* A Review of Poetry, Prose & Art—at
www.ablemuse.com

Able Muse Press
467 Saratoga Avenue #602
San Jose, CA 95129

Acknowledgments

I am grateful to the editors of the following journals where many of these poems originally appeared, sometimes in slightly different forms:

Able Muse: "The Eviction," "Obituary," and "Song: Post Mortem"

Autumn Sky: "Song: Go and Do It"

Cimarron Review: "The Next Epiphany" and "Where I Am"

The Dark Horse: "The Queen of France"

Don't Talk to Me about Love: "Song: Defiantly of Love" and "The Only Way"

The New Criterion: "Happy Birthday, Herod"

Peacock Journal: "A Memory Perhaps"

Rattle: "Divertimento"

Smartish Pace: "Blizzard Bird," *"Le cirque douteux,"* "Galapagos Now," and "The Undersigned"

Times Literary Review: "My Political Poem"

IN *MANHATTANITE,* HIS SECOND BOOK of poems, Aaron Poochigian takes on the role of American flâneur for the twenty-first century, drifting through the frenetic metropolis at a dreamer's planetary pace. This collection is a celebration of exuberant melancholy, or melancholy exuberance, slick lyric cum urbane pastoral. I say "exuberant" because despite the themes of loneliness and isolation, Poochigian's verse is never taciturn: like a Broadway musical, it is always bursting into song, not only reveling in rhyme (and reason), but even refrain. Poochigian's is a tuneful solitude.

That the poet's "day job" is as a Classical translator (Poochigian is probably best known for his Sappho), an exacting calling that paradoxically demands compromise at every turn, the fitting of sound to an extant and sometimes alien sense, may account for the sensation of freedom—the hooky or holiday giddiness—of Poochigian in his own poetry. The professor has been let loose to play. Thus, in a single poem, we might find congeries of words such as "Murphy's Oil Soap," "schlep," "déjà vu," and "rugged household gods." Poochigian rhymes "bodega" with "Omega," "End" with "and."

While Poochigian, like Sappho, writes a mean love poem, the most romantic—and exotic—word in *Manhattanite* turns out to be "Ohio," with its sighing *h* flanked by *O*'s of delight and surprise. We might in turn supply "Poet" in the place of its apostrophe: "Thank you, Ohio, for reminding me/ How Art should astound."

—A. E. Stallings, 2016 Able Muse Book Award judge,
author of *Olives*

Contents

III. The Middle of It All

IV. Characters

V. Defiantly of Love

Manhattanite

I. The Next Epiphany

Take It to the Roof

It's crazy that the tipsy gravitate
toward precipices, but they do, they do:
the high love highness; an ecstatic state
defies the nag of earth. We knew (we *knew*)

but, caution nonsense to communal stupor,
up we went and stormed the rooftop, feeling
primitive, propounding, *Screw the super!*
Wake the neighbors! Crack the penthouse ceiling!

Since two hands (like, my own or someone else's)
had brought the tunes, our would-be-airborne corps
had found its wind and synchronized its pulses,
and more came spilling through the fire door, more

evaporated in the dervish blur.
Oblivion! That's what it's like in groups;
that's how it is with liquor. If there were
some clumsy jostlers and a few sad droops,

we were, in concert, still one oversexed
amoebic beast sublimely throbbing, bending
the guardrail gulfward, and. . . . What happened next
eludes the conscious mind, so, for an ending,

I came round Sunday on a floor of doubt,
grateful whatever blitz that bacchanal
had brought about had goddamn gone all-out,
exploding, for a spell, my in-di-vid-u-al.

Him

The roof at 2 a.m.; a plastic chair
beside a low brick ledge: terrestrial cars
will not stop bleating on the thoroughfare;
that shimmer overhead is not the stars

but too much city, too much city light.
Eight days the heat wave has refused to break.
My antique fan has broke down out of spite;
my shower: broke. Way more than I can take,

and now, this . . . wow: a breeze, a taste of rain.
Thank you, whatever sent them. I don't know,
what drives the wind that spins the weather vane?
Some oomph, I guess, some sort of dynamo

out there enacting atmospheric laws.
Something must power such, like, grand machines—
some primal force, a source, a cosmic cause,
the Yes emitting everywhere, which means

Was I a long time wrong? Was I the fraud?
Big drops are falling, and the atheist
that did his best is melting. Oh my God,
my God, this weather feels like you exist.

Autumnal

The sweatered walk with coffee cups in hand.
A baby stirs beneath synthetic layers.
Calmly a cop stamps, calmly speed-chess players
blow on their hands and move. A hotdog stand,
because it breathes, is steaming up the air.
We all make cloud in concert, even me,
a denim near-invisibility,
puffing a slantwise course across the square.

I love you, Fall, you chipper interim
between the hostile heat-waves and the grim
term when we keep inside and curse the weather.

I love you for the way you slow things down
and for the way you make me love this town
so much that random people seem together.

Blizzard Bird

This brilliant blight that built up overnight,
the Seagull-of-the-City-under-Snow,
is not his own fowl, but the town's, the weather's.
He wears our streets as streaks across his feathers
and, when we say *goddamn nor'easters* blow,
we mean the motion of his wings in flight.

The subway rumbling underneath the white
is dimly rumbling through his hollow bones,
but up here only squints can blunt the glare:
when his electric lashings zap the air,
flags flagrantly convulse, and traffic cones
stand for him when his saffron legs alight.

Doomed, though, like ice is doomed, this wicked bright
Seagull Behemoth soon must furl his gusts
and die the same slow way the drifts accrued,
like mad ambition, like a winter mood,
when revolutions cut him down to crusts
and vision settles gentler on the sight.

The Undersigned

Six zigzag flights, and all that you have been
becomes a key, that turns. A door swings in
and, *Wow,* a promenade of burled and burnished
cherry is airing Murphy's Oil Soap.
What with the fresh whitewash, the whole unfurnished
tenement sports an airbrush sheen of hope.

*Too bad this magic box, this cramped but vast
potential, can't quite disappear the past.*

The tenant prior, now a wire coat-hanger,
dangles in place of drapery; plaster fill
pockmarks the hollow walls his private anger
horse-kicked and sucker-punched. The windowsill
exhibits interlocking evidence
of bottles' bottoms. Gunk congests the vents.

You feel that doom; you left some remnants, too.
A schlep down Bowery, and your déjà-vu
boxes will hump the steps and cram Cloud Nine
with choice leftovers from the chance before.
The paint will chip, then chip some more; the shine
expire when gimcrack traffic scuffs the floor.

*You get how visions swindle, but the scam
just keeps on gleaming from beyond the jamb.*

Yeah, stuffed with grub and rugged household gods,
this cube of heaven will be coop enough
to call an island when your outside odds
melt into one big oceanic bluff.
Step in, with shoes on. You have signed your name.
Maybe this time the dream won't end the same.

Where I Am

The staggered maples come
running along the path
southbound, and in the south,
like someone in a dream,
I'm jogging where I am.

A sparrow swooping by
has up and struck my chest.
A rotten fence has thrust
a picket at my knee.
All things converge on me.

Under a rhythmic sun
parked cars accelerate
toward me down the street.
A speeding traffic sign
flares orange and is gone.

Midway: a cul-de-sac
has spun about my hand.
Creation goes around,
and what arrived comes back
retrograde, block by block.

Sight, like a movie screen,
revisits the advance
of squirrel and picket fence.
I huff, a constant man,
taking the movement in.

The same hypnotic frame
replays the little wood,
the gate, my neighborhood.
My stoop recurs, my home
returns to where I am.

Obituary

You, passing stranger, as you walk this walk,
around you see bodegas, vendors, kiosks,
stairwells to trains arriving every minute,
a cityscape a long time fully grown
with, sad at last, a poster-boarded diner,
a place of failure, soon to be reborn
as something flashy. Thirty years it served
Americana-for-the-budget-patron—
PB&J, pork roast and mashed potatoes,
that kind of thing. The loss of it is marked
by playbills and a rental agent's number.

And what of those that worked there? Well, the owner
sold off the salamanders, griddle, frier,
even the clock, and bought a Sport Clips franchise;
the grizzled waitress moved in with a son;
one sous-chef went on to prepare new specials
at Burger King. As for the rest, who knows?

Keep walking, stranger. Change is often tragic,
and who can grieve for every good thing gone?
This passing notice is already done.

The Recidivist

This Wednesday Stephen, seven weeks confined
for getting busted wasted at the wheel,
will bus back home to face a dry ordeal
again. He just might leave the curse behind.

Yes, after terrorizing humankind
he found religion. He will weep and kneel.
May he withstand the bottle's dark appeal.
May he maintain a Purgatory mind.

We, too, are burdened: we must not be blind
to lies and lapses as we watch him heal.
Certainly he could now stay straight for real.
We all must struggle not to be resigned.

Oh Stephen, charming Stephen, much maligned
Stephen, my blessings on this bout of zeal—
but, damn it, doubts are circling, and I feel
helpless to catch the crash I have divined.

The Next Epiphany

Streetlights blossom as the sun goes down.
A brown rat rises from a sewer drain.
A shot goes pop and echoes; spiral sirens
pass into what could pass for silence.
A bright bridge and the towers beyond it stand
for all there is
of hope in this metropolis,
an aging body with a modern mind.

Hung up on all or nothing, now or never,
I'm out this evening walking by the river
among the rubbish, aching to divine
some further sign inside the scene.
Another crazy searching for religion
in stray newspapers,
bottles, bags, and candy wrappers,
I stalk Manhattan like a grizzled pigeon.

What revelation can exalt this mess?
I hear an engine churning and the hiss
of woken foam: an endless garbage scow
is nosing level with me now.
I wave; a horn replies. Tonight's the night:
fields of *basura*
are glowing in the holy aura
issuing from the pilot's Midas light.

I asked for vision, and a vision came
out of the urban twilight like a dream.
Who needs a shower of gold? Who needs the moon?
I am beholden to the riverman
whose lamp has made my evening walk along
an asphalt path
a journey toward the sort of faith
that holds for here and now and vibes like song.

Song: Post Mortem

Although I can see her still
above the cutting board
mincing ginger and dill,
and now she is leaning toward
my lips in candlelight,
and we have moved to the bed,
and she will spend the night,
that girl, *my* girl, is dead.

(Not dead:
just married to *him* instead.)

Although we are holding hands
while walking after dark
past cupcake and souvenir stands
on the edge of Central Park,
and the roused red mulberry trees
are rustling overhead
when I get on my knees,
that girl, *my* girl, is dead.

(Not dead:
just married to *him* instead.)

For all that by chance today
near Macy's on Fulton Mall,
while scuffing along on my way
to a one-room hole-in-the-wall,
I saw her with sons in tow,
and, yes, her hair is as red
as twenty years ago,
that girl, *my* girl, is dead.

(Not dead:
just married to *him* instead.)

The Great Escape

The country childhood she is running from
receding like a bruise, our ingénue
slogs through a leech- and slug-infested slough,
scrabbles up to a road and jabs her thumb
at elsewhere eyes. High-school opprobrium
like hellfire heartens her the whole night through.
When asked at daybreak where she's headin' to,
she smiles big, welcoming the life to come.

The oracles are mum;
the rules, untrue—
no way to get a clue.
Don't crumple; don't go numb.
The best may happen to you.

After a lifetime in a dreamy slum
what struck her most is passing in review:
rock dove eruptions; a construction crew
hooting as she sashays; that raving bum
who used a trashcan as a kettledrum;
smashed bottles, kittens—urban residue.
She dies then, smiling, ready to pursue
that next great getaway, the life to come.

The oracles are mum;
the rules, untrue—
no way to get a clue.
Don't crumple; don't go numb.
The best may happen to you.

II. The Traveler

The Drive

Coyote eyes ignite. A near, then nearer
pair of white lights passes with a flash
and dwindles, crimson, in the rearview mirror.
The center line is going dash, dash, dash.

Night has caught my little lime-green Ford
in desert country, halfway in-between
what went to Hell and what I'm heading toward.
All I've got now is this, like, bleary scene

spooling along outside of Nowheresville.
The dashboard clock is reading miles to go.
My toes are pressuring the pedal. Still,
velocity has never gone so slow.

What if the jinx just keeps on catching me?
What if the same mess bubbles up again?
This fresh redemptive opportunity
would go down ugly. No big hurry, then.

I ease the seat back, let up on the gas.
The wheels of angst less desperately spin.
I switch the air off, ravel down the glass.
Essence of silver sagebrush rushes in.

Better to think my future is improving
with every mile I travel from that town.
Someday I will be through with all this moving.
Somewhere my luck will up and settle down.

Turf

Here in the strangeness you are straying through,
a citron hawk is yawping as he wheels,
fluorescent moss is yielding to your heels,
and trilliums are blooming where the Sioux
lie heaped in barrows. Even death is new.
Go stroke that pine, feel how the resin feels . . .
Manhattanite, your touching awe reveals
how otherworldly nature's been to you.

There's no bodega, zoo or high-rise here—
a broken moldering birch, like déjà vu;
like déjà vu, that grove alive with deer
and squirrels, flying squirrels. Amnesiac,
why is this forest like a place you knew?
Not Central Park, but deeper, further back.

Divertimento

There had been no attraction, no surprise
for fifty miles, just crows, Holsteins and stubble,
and now, atop the only local rise,
like an ungatherable

iron flower, this looky-here wind turbine.
Sure, it turns a hair-harassing day
to zaps that, routed eastward, power urban
transit, say,

or crab canneries further up the coast,
but in this yawner of a Bronze-Age Now,
among the ruminants, what matters most
is just, like, freaking wow—

Bravissimo for the kinetic sculpture
dangling upward from a snag of earth
while juggling, with acquiescent rapture,
three arms' worth

of gale-force wind. Oh yeah, I wanna be
that gleam with crazy feelers going round.
Thank you, Ohio, for reminding me
how Art should astound.

A Memory, Perhaps

Light rain; an ultra-modern train
lisping through French or German woods.
Beyond the wide-screen windowpane
gypsies are camping near the tracks—
their clothes earthy as oaks, their hoods
burlap. One brings a blur of axe

down on a birch branch, down again;
another cooking at a fire
rips feathers from a headless hen;
the rest, though, have convened around
the zither-man, a solo choir,
chanting a saga, without sound . . .

mushrooms have sprouted from the log
his staunchest fans are sitting on;
a child is crying; a rangy dog
is head-down licking chicken scraps.
Then tunnel dark: the glimpse has gone
back into memory, perhaps.

Galapagos Now

Guide gone, the stutter of a trail
I turned to turned to gully, cut
a no man's gash through shell and shale
and died just shy of reeking what?

A sump? A swamp? A green and hairy
goulash of a secret slough?
Rival gropes of topiary
strained the sunlight. What got through

confided, writhing on the surface,
some deep beast's lithe extremity,
its nib an optic nub that, nervous,
throbbed in awe of plain old me.

Plunk, and the scope was sunken; bubbles
glug-glug-gasped and, as if charmed,
what scrummage of Abominables
rose from ooze? What lemur-armed

amoebas lapped in furs of germs?
What zebras flapping stingray wings?
What feathered eels? What pulsing worms
bipedal? What ungodly *things?*

No way that lot had proper parents.
The stew's dark virtues must have spawned
miracles of bizarre aberrance
and reared them there, beyond Beyond.

Eureka! but, a meek explorer,
I shrieked and bolted—in my mind
the horror of it, my own horror,
one fanged feeler's length behind. . . .

That tale of course was total hooey,
but, damn, one whiff of rot or fen,
and the whole palpitating gooey
rhapsody bubbles up again.

Cinéma pur

All I did was ease
my eyelids and, *Whoa,* a lurking
art film had begun:

the Guide, the God, the One,
a skeleton
in top hat and opera cape,
his pointer finger jerking
through three hundred sixty degrees
of black-and-white desertscape,

and a hero stuck astraddle
an ostrich without reins—
halves of a warring whole
ungalloping the gains
they make toward no fixed goal,

and the dearth of depth and shadow
under eternal noon,
and the sandstorm soon
to expunge their preposterous quest
forever moving in
from north, south, east or west . . .

all started in the middle
and never rolled *The End.*
No Sphinx in the thing, no riddle,
just dunes and doom and *and.*

The Child of Fortune

Daily since waking I had galloped nearer
some goal I simply knew was mine out there:
Snowflower, Riddle's Answer, Talking Mirror
or, say, Rapunzel letting down her hair.

Yep, me and Mule, hilarious alliance,
ran with the koans of clairvoyant crones,
threaded the pendulums of tramping giants
and cheated trolls with trails of chicken bones

but now, just past a last ramshackle bridge,
the trophy winking from the witch's tower
climactic there beyond a final ridge
has lost, with nearness, its bewitching power.

Mule has hunkered down and won't press on.
A crosswind sniffs my quandary. Lone clouds pass.
The pilot spirit of my days is gone,
and I am drifting in a pool of grass.

There will be peace, there will be panic now,
since freedom means the will to choose *who knows?*
A mill beside a stream, a sturdy Frau,
brood chickens, philosophical repose.

872 South Fowler

I.

A moldboard plow with creepy-moustache tines;
a drunken toolshed rocking in suspense;
fire-hazard heaps of brush and lumber; vines
derelict masters of a backyard fence

breached here and there to let the rabbits in;
old orange trees the squirrels have gotten to;
Bermuda grass like moss; a cracked, has-been
veranda; an umbrella pole off true;

a twice kicked-in, twice reinforced back door;
that wedding portrait on the shelf, their eyes;
non-burgled knick-knacks; chandeliers galore
dangling webs of ghostly length and size;

a tasseled lamp; a Cupid-tastic vase;
a wide-screen reprint full of Chartres and sheep—
no thief or squatter checking out the place,
only an heir with nowhere else to sleep;

a bedroom where the urban Bedouin
can wake to swan's down slowly, day by day;
a household where Contentment can begin
urging, among the birdsong, *Why not stay?*

II.
After Manhattan and the sacred rage
my love is now a broken-down garage
pockmarked by buckshot. I will leave the heap
the way it is. Outside, a netless hoop
is waiting for a dunk that never comes.
Inside, much rubbish: V-dub pushrod cams,
pull chains for fans. That viperous vacuum tube
will never wriggle from its rubber tub
to breathe again. If ousted, I will miss
even the oil spill, possum nest and mess
of spider webs.
                    All round the shambles grass
luxuriates unmowed—a state of grace
like freedom, like a hardcore hobo's hair.
How nice that nothing ever happens here.
I mean, just past the posts and razor wire,
those ducklings dabbling in the reservoir
would sooner pass unknown. That's how this lawn,
this shed are happy to be left alone.

III. The Middle of It All

My Political Poem

Election Night. A Walmart parking lot.
A green fog off the half-drained reservoir
had jumped the fence to breed with puffs of pot
issuing from a mag-wheeled muscle car.
Like always, sick of work by eight o'clock,
I had gone out and squatted on my knees
among the dumpsters near the loading dock
to feed a pack of strays. The runt Burmese
that goes by Freak was up on lizard hips
licking the gravy from my fingertips.
So cute—one-eyed, scab-nostriled, stumpy-tailed.

Because, whichever rancid sack prevailed,
that evening meant, like, *Fuck you all—The End,*
civic seppuku, the Apocalypse,
I guess I itched for something, some hushed friend
too innocent to be American.
Everywhere gobs of noise just wouldn't quit:
a speaker-mounted Wrangler nagging *Vote!,*
fireworks like gunshots, bleats, gunshots again. . . .

I grabbed my mutant future by the throat
and wrestled it, a squall of snag and spit,
into the footwell of my shotgun seat.
The whole drive home I wept to hear it cry
as blood ran loving down my wrists and chest.
Sorry, so sorry: it was for the best.

What had to happened, and a week went by,
and she and I, domestic in our way,
are settling into a full retreat:
I sit and write my little songs all day;
she chases toys across the kitchen floor
and down the slippery hardwood to our door,
our big new door, the barrier I pray
will prove enough to keep America at bay.

Tragique

Beau idéal of dash and discipline,
the latest Czech takes up his violin,
plucks a ridiculously chipper chord
and jigs a bit about the fingerboard
before glissading, *molto pensivo,*
into the very Tartarus of woe
where star-crossed lovers and the *misérables*
make hay of life's unfairness—*keen, gasp, sob.*
We all sit up and, dragged down where they are,
savor the anguish like a chocolate bar.

Never was misery so beautiful,
never—it's not like that. It is a dull
distancing or a self-destructive shove,
a rancid thing that doesn't move like love.
Music, you slick mythmaker, you beguiling
excitement, will you get away with styling
wretchedness as the acme of romance?

(My God, it's gorgeous how the tragic dance
goes graveward trailing tatters of tristesse.)

Soon as he plucks us back to perkiness
and saws *The End,* I blort *Bravo! Encore!*
He made depression something to adore—
mere fantasy, mere fiction. I want more.

Round the World

Light is ending; dark ascending:
hours loud in human sight
here are long past, and the long last
shadows ripening toward night.

Muted little noncommittal
creatures poised in cleft and nest
peep and rally, brave the alley.
Batwings adumbrate unrest.

East is all in; West has fallen.
Now the horned owl's turret glare
tracks a starling, and the darling
tabby guts a hobbled hare.

Still the diverse meek survivors
go on grubbing for their needs;
still some living wombs are giving
vermin birth among the weeds.

Dark is ending; light ascending:
black rats, pack rats, moles and voles
hazard travel over gravel
back into their hidey-holes.

Then the omen comes, a gnomon
child stilt-shadowed in the dawn,
flinging news of inconclusive
clashes where our night has gone.

Uneventful

An adenoidal tortoiseshell is snoring
next to me on a tired green ottoman.
Outside the picture window there's the lawn
with grackles hopping on it. Now and then
dog-walkers. Cars go by, each one a yawn.
There were some workmen with a mixer pouring
cement for someone's curb, but they are gone.
The crosstown bus has come around again.

So what? You say. *Why document the boring?*

Because I want to keep that afternoon—
the one I spent delectably ignoring,
Good God, incessant tragic goings-on—
separate forever as a vault of Zen.
Plane crash, mass murder, terminal typhoon
are real out there and *live!* on CNN,
brash on my laptop, crawling down my phone.
Though I would never ask to be immune
to other people's fortunes, or my own,
there will be crises when I will be keen
to slip inside the circle I have drawn
around a perfectly unshocking scene.

IV. Characters

The Chromatist

Large on the bench, the lord of torque
fillips the wooden music stand
with his resplendent witching fork,
smiles at the vibe and wrings the A's
till their aberrant throbbings find,
after intensest strain, release.

Yes, what this old piano wants
is harmony of hertz and guts,
and the arbiter of consonance
gets what the wires are twanging toward—
a warmth of notes among the notes,
a colorscape more felt than heard.

Soon as his gentle wrench and pliers
tease out the complete solfège,
triumph as grand as many choirs
emanates without cringe or damper
from a hunk of wood and a man on stage
with an empty hall for an echo chamber.

The Changeling

On days when debt, rent, bus or dying car
so rack our self-worth that we feel we are
nobility which a neonatal switch
has shunted into Hell,
we would do well
to think on Stanislav Romanovich,
unsung successor to a gutted tsar:

though armed with fobs and clippings that could prove
his ticker pumped the richest Romanov,
he kept it real, drove taxi in Bayonne
ate Spam and ran on Folgers
while Bolshie soldiers
knocked back stuff that should have been his own.
Nah, nah, for Stan, strong coffee was enough—

enough when the United Front had grown
shabby and nabbed an Occupation Zone,
enough when grumps would not stop playing chess
with men like missile launchers.
Stan picked the Dodgers
over a fireside Fabergé noblesse
and outrage pure as fission, pure as bone.

The Rajah of Rout

Losing its grappling hold
on facts and family, the old
wrestler's broken brain
registers too much cold
always and, somewhere, pain.

The beefcake that made him proud
shivering under a shawl—
a stenciled robe? a shroud?—
the vagueness of it all
coheres at times as a crowd
that roars when he roars from the wings
in flame-embroidered tights,
the hush when the fight bell rings,
the actual rage that grows
from bogus body blows,
or the view of the stadium lights
from face up on the mat.

(The count is on, *one, two* . . . ,
like fate, like déjà vu.)

Though he has gone to fat,
the blustery past that persists
inside him wants to shout:
"I am the Rajah of Rout!
The Hammer, the Slammer, the Smother,
His Lordship Look-Out-Brother-
Death-Is-in-These-Fists!"

Every Sunday night
a daughter he takes for his mother
joins the strapping men
that strut through his reverie.
She plays along, strokes his hair,
glad he is unaware
of the drag-out, knock-down fight
from which it's fixed that (. . . *three!*)
he won't get up again.

Le cirque douteux

Left from the last step, past the laundry room,
a bare bulb noirs the cell to which I doom
all that I can't accept and won't let go
(a dungeon, yes, but less Guantanamo
than Mental Ward). The current roster boasts
Swampthing and Bigfoot, vampires, banshees, ghosts,
the Rebel Angel and the Whirlwind God.

Don't worry, these celebrities of fraud
will never come to trial, and that's the point:
to keep the freaks on ice in one snug joint
so I, Mad Hatter at our talent shows,
can zing tomatoes when the spooks expose
Adidas underneath their sheets, a mute
stilt walker sweats through his gorilla suit
or, worse, the Serpent yodels backward psalms.
I weep when Awesome too overtly palms
the locusts hidden up His itchy sleeve.

If now unwound and reason proved naïve,
the boys would overrun the bluegrass, fill
neighborhoods, nations, continents until
the whole world thrilled again with fright and magic.

If I could come of age, a quick untragic
ax would euthanize their painful gags,
my modest lawn be morgue to body bags,
my mind hygienic, and the hole bricked in.

Meanwhile the clowns are stuck what they have been—
nightly attractions half inside, half out,
the spotlight shadows of a vaudeville doubt.

Blatant

A banner gallivanting in the breeze,
a serpentine impertinently bright,
a perfectly bravura streak of tease
leapt through my pupils to the seat of sight
exclaiming:

> *Yoo-hoo. Here I am. Delight*
> *in me. I am, of all idolatries,*
> *least subtle. All I say I say outright.*
> *Equivocations? Hidden meanings? Please!*
> *I flap and ripple, sometimes hang at ease—*
> *that's it. Orange, I am black-and-white.*

I squinted like a man whose squint would seize
something elusive, something recondite.

Derelicts

I.
I heard the harmless maniac
who camps in front of my bodega
roar from his carton on the stoop:
"I am the Alpha and Omega,
the kick in the smack, the massive attack,
the zoom bah bah, zoom bah; whoop, whoop, whoop!"

Polychrome Christmas lights were blinking.
A white dove—well, alright, a pigeon—
posed on the guy's cardboard façade.
I don't go in much for religion
but, trust me, I could not help thinking,
"Lo, another son of God."

II.
I love you, wacko, with my own self-love

because I see myself there sleeping rough
on cardboard under a construction scaffold.
Because I hear my future in your cough,

my voice among your three defiant voices,
I love you, wacko, with my own self-love.
What crisis crazed you? Was it chance or choices?

Come summer, if my doom does not improve,
Manhattan will resound with *me* unraveled.
So here's a buck—a fiver? That's enough:

I love you, wacko, with my own self-love.

III.
Ah, where the wind is ruffling
trash bags, and moonlight snags
on cracked façades: that shuffling,
nebulous humanoid
who glooms through shreds and drags
a shadow like a void.

The beards of the Unemployed
  dissolve in the rags
  and shag of night.

Mott Street, each time I walk it,
parades this mental case.
Last week he dredged his pocket,
flashed me a watch—no band,
just a smashed, digital face.
The time: *Please Understand.*

A whirlpool demand
  from backward space;
  a black-hole wound.

He always gives me this funny
feeling, a pity akin
to rage: should I toss money
into a bottomless bum?
Indulge my nagging twin?
Feed what I could become?

Here's something, Mr. Mum,
but keep your grin—
I don't want none.

IV.
It's late and lost in tunnels that I find him—
Mr. Mirror Shades (the mufflered one),
his past the tentacles of pipes behind him,
his stature like a hunched harp made of bone.

A tarot card, a king of prophecy
enthroned on coats and rubbish, he sometimes
rattles his wicked little cup my way
and conjures up a mishegoss of rhymes:

> *One wave of poison, two of disease,*
> *and a pulse will roast your phones and freeze*
>   *your engines.*
> *Rats, then, will rise through the sewer grates*
> *as executors for the Fiend or Fates*
>   *and gnaw with a vengeance.*

> *Sirens will sing the Apocalypse Blues*
> *and, morning, noon, and night, the news*
>   *will be static.*
> *Why bother dialing nine-one-one?*
> *Why dash for the drawer and get out the gun?*
>   *Why hide in the attic?*

No one will be surviving this,
so go out and find somebody to kiss,
*   or religion.*
A blood tide creeping up our shores,
it's time to get down with the dinosaurs
*   and passenger pigeon.*

So he intones, out of his nose, his *skull.*
Chuckling, then, he scrunches for a bow,
and I give something to the oracle
for briefly making Armageddon now.

Mr. Vigilant

Atop a pillar like an alpine peak
the lion-tousled, limestone patriarch
(for all that he might lack of vital spark)
is heeding: snow is falling; cedars creak.
A streetlight throws a circle of mystique
about him. He is never in the dark.
He hubs the spokes of a concentric park.
A cold wind blows the urban landscape bleak.

If he unfroze, what would his ache remark?

Leaves, give me leaves—these trees are branch and bark.
Give me some children playing hide-and-seek.
Here at the crux of daylight's losing streak,
sure, there are pigeons, but I miss the lark,
the mime, the picnic.
                        If his look could speak.

Song: The Queen of France

For the Cirque Rouge Cabaret

The backlot was a royal garden.
Dolls made up my court:
the pretty ones were granted pardon;
the ugly hanged for sport.

Tyrant at ten I was the glory
of soaring tenements,
trumpeting, "On your knees before me—
I am the Queen of France."

Let all chandeliers burst into tears
and no stallions prance—
it's been thirty years
since I was Queen of France.

Common things broke in like rebels,
denying my sovereign right.
Riches now are tips on tables,
and exile the spotlight

where I pose in rags Parisian,
teaching a guttural throng
(for the pittance of admission)
how Time did me wrong.

Let all chandeliers burst into tears
and no stallions prance—
it's been thirty years
since I was Queen of France.

Let long gawps from the upper tier
invade my bustier,
and lowlifes dangling dollars cheer
for my constricted sway,

with will unweathered and a manner
proud when I come unfurled,
I shall remain a brilliant banner
and rampart to the world.

V. Defiantly of Love

Song: Go and Do It

Leap Niagara, ask a Mountie
where they keep the *joie de vivre,*
then cruise down to Orange County,
surf the curl and smoke some reefer.
Ride class fives in the Cascades,
water-ski the Everglades,
    go, go, go
    until you know
precisely where the Good Times flow.

Hitchhike through the heartland, travel
wide, acquire a taste for tillage.
Where the asphalt turns to gravel
settle down in some quaint village—
cloudy, clear or partly sunny,
your new Land of Milk and Honey
    will appear
    much like here
but less suburban, more sincere.

Search through endless desert places
for the perfect little spot.
When at last some plush oasis
tallies with the spa you sought,
think of me and write a letter
gloating over how much better
    life is there—
    I'll still swear
we could be happy anywhere.

Ménage à deux

I.
That night of excess
the half that was she
said yes, yes, yes
to me, to me

as we, a smother
of grunt and scent,
each sought in the other
a complement.

And it worked: in the act
one breath, one skin,
we reached what we lacked;
we took it in.

Sex in the past
had been something to do;
but this, this at last
was something new.

A fateful heave,
and we lay in the dark
like Adam and Eve
back in the Park.

When we woke next day
it was understood
we ought to stay
conjoined for good.

II.
Stomping in winter boots across the square,
and Isa weeping. This would be the scene
where I refused, she ranted, and the glare
ice turned to slush beneath us. The wind was mean,
but I was brutal. She was all I had,
a wounded monster dying in the wild,
and Love had done it. Love had made us sad
crude halves that never would be reconciled.

The Only Way

When Mister Right has strayed so far you hate him,
pluck a wild leek from peat-rich soil
and eat the stalk before you go to bed.

Spit thrice at sunrise, bathe and scratch, verbatim,
this lethal summons into kitchen foil:
"Vengeance, go find him, bind him guts, heart, head.

Compel the traitor, no will of his own,
into my bedroom to be mine till death.
Should rival hags assail him, make him fail

to function, make him pleasure me alone—
KALOU KAGOEI BAINA-BAINAKETH."
Roll up the love charm, pierce it with a nail,

and seed it in a field where fireweed
attests to ashes. With the next moonrise
he will arrive, the lover you deserve,

less work than when you knew him, guaranteed
to lock you, goddess, in his zombie eyes
and sate your spite with almost human verve.

Least Eligible

1.
They left a gash that day, the bride and groom.

Their whole thing blossomed out of cyberspace:
flirtations under witty *noms de plume*
spilled over to a Starbucks. Face to face,
they knew, just *knew.* No lies, no dodge-and-chase.
A few days later, in the afterglow
of Ipswich oysters and a Broadway show,
they found each other easy to embrace
and . . . no more details needed. (I assume
what's known as "love" was falling into place.)
Still worse, years in, the usual spousal gloom
has failed to wilt their hothouse nuptial bloom.
They live and breathe affection. Way to go.
Thoughts of them always lead to *maybe . . . No.*

2.
Out of that kneejerk, negative command,
an image surfaces to plug the hurt:
a hermit clad in rags and crud, unshod,
his beard in dreads. He wears no wedding band.
Sometimes he tramps around a world of dirt
hunting up gushers with a witching rod;
sometimes he feeds coyotes from his hand;
most often, kneeling in a nylon yurt,
he venerates a lumpish little god
that means, for him, all beauty, all romance.

A guy like that—don't say he missed his chance.

The Vacca

A long-legged Golden Calf
is god of this wilderness,
and me and my Bedouin boys
laugh and sing, sing and laugh
all night in pious excess
because the god loves noise.

And the old is new again.
Amen. Amen.

A mule train down a ravine,
and we kneel at the altar of
a mutilated cliff
where grazes, amid obscene
professions of deathless love,
a bovine petroglyph.

And the old is new again.
Amen. Amen.

What should a man profess?
How choose among higher powers?
Whatever godling moves
a soul to sing, I guess.
You have yours; we have ours,
and ours has little hooves.

And the old is new again.
Amen. Amen.

Here she is—diamond-eyed,
all sass and holy glow—
a luscious load to laud.
We can't stop stroking her hide,
can't stop repeating *O*
my darling, O my God.

And the old is new again.
Amen. Amen.

Happy Birthday, Herod

Like always, Herod's birthday is today,
and I can hear the tambourine
brioso. I can hear the oboe skirl.
Like always, Salome
is getting down to business, veil by veil.
Her eyes are green;
all other eyes, obscene
ravishers of a writhing girl,
are piercing what is see-through anyway.

Like always, without fail,
something repulsive has been done:
under the Dead Sea sun
another sort of flesh
(that corpse I mean, the headless one)
is summoning the blowflies—fresh
gratification for a mother's grudge.

Like always, who am I to judge?
Indifferent to whatever moral thing
a servant might be carrying
around the party on a tray,
I stand with stiff voyeurs
devouring those curves of hers,
worshipping the elastic,
the orgastic,
Salome.

Forgive me: Herod's birthday is today.

One Too Many

My raucous ex, Alexa Glossolalia,
has up and made off with my mouth again.
Yep, yep, this yap, her pretty little Polly, a
megaphone for a mad comedienne.

Lord, may the spastic waggling of my tongue
strike all their earsies as divine. Amen.
My larynx laughs; I hear that laughter sung.
Oh God, Oh God, the music of a hen.

Why beef *this freak ain't me, my basso burr*
would never have agreed to tweak like this?
My claque would roar the more if I charged her
with fucking up a good man's drunkenness.

Nah, when ecstatic blab is holding sway,
it's no use getting pissy. Best dismiss
this selfish business of a sober say
and, dummyhead, succumb to dummy bliss.

The Eviction

I gave the knob a good loud rattle
to tell whatever critters
were in there, please, to run and hide.
With that, I threw the front door wide.
We heard no skitters.

But, wow, what guilt: the family chattel
wore the dust
Neglect deposits, as it must,
on all that goes neglected.
Interconnected,
innocence-entangling
vertigos of webwork ran
from escritoire to ottoman.
Caught moths were dangling,
mummified, like ornaments.

Agony to have to reclaim
by rag and broom
the fancy living room
I had consigned to decadence
for decades. All the same,
the time had come to teach the spiders
this wasn't their inheritance
to build on as they pleased.
We were the new insiders,
and we had come to stay.

You laughed. I sneezed—
a sign, perhaps, that we should start
ripping the intricate
disgrace apart
and whisking it
in tatters out of doors.

Respectful in a way,
we labored silently to sate,
if it was not too late,
the nagging of my ancestors.

Song: Defiantly of Love

Meet her at Grand Central Station
and walk her down under the bridge
where the wild kids play in the street all day
and your neighbor, a passionate Haitian,
sings ecstatically, ecstatically, ecstatically of love.

Feed her potatoes au gratin,
meatloaf and corn on the cob
when the couple upstairs quarrels and swears,
and all the rats in Manhattan
sing discordantly, discordantly, discordantly of love.

Worship her like a religion,
like Mary the Mother of God,
while he-dogs compete for a she-dog in heat
and a lonesome crippled pigeon
sings obsessively, obsessively, obsessively of love.

Promise to love her forever
and always, come what may,
while the basso bum with his bottle of rum
and the post-industrial river
sing defiantly, defiantly, defiantly of love.

Aaron Poochigian earned a PhD in Classics from the University of Minnesota in 2006 and an MFA in Poetry from Columbia University in 2016. His book of translations from Sappho, *Stung With Love,* was published by Penguin Classics in 2009, and his translation of Apollonius's *Jason and the Argonauts* was released October 2014. For his work in translation he was awarded a 2010–2011 Grant by the National Endowment for the Arts. His first book of original poetry, *The Cosmic Purr* (Able Muse Press) was  published in 2012, and several of the poems in it collectively won the New England Poetry Club's Daniel Varoujan Prize. His work has appeared in *The Guardian, Poems Out Loud,* and *Poetry.*

photo by Sumner Hatch

ALSO FROM ABLE MUSE PRESS

www.ablemusepress.com

CPSIA information can be obtained
at www.ICGtesting.com
Printed in the USA
LVOW12s1637150717
540935LV00005B/8/P